Composting

How Organic Gardeners Let it Rot and Make Homegrown Humus

Gaia Rodale

Gaia Rodale

Just to say Thank You for Purchasing this Book, I want
to give you a gift <u>100% absolutely FREE</u>

A Copy of My Upcoming Special Report "The Organic
Gardener's Calendar: Monthly 'To-Do's' for Beginner
Gardeners"

Go to <u>www.OrganicPlantingGuides.com</u>
to Reserve Your FREE Copy Today.

Table of Contents

Introduction

I want to thank you and congratulate you for purchasing, *"How Organic Gardeners Let it Rot and Make Homegrown Humus."*

For an organic gardener, a backyard compost pile offers two major benefits. First, it creates a free, organic soil amender that is known to improve soil structure and help produce hearty, healthy plants. Second, it cuts back on the gardener's environmental footprint by recycling about 30% of the material they would be sending to a landfill. When you factor in all the other great things about composting, it is definitely a win-win-win.

Composting takes nature's way of recycling organic matter and gives it a boost. By creating the ideal conditions for decomposition, composting systems speed up the process, turning kitchen scraps and yard waste into high-quality humus in a matter of weeks. This humus can then be used to amend the soil, which increases its ability to hold water and nutrients.

This guide provides you with the basic information you need to start your own composting system. From explaining how composting works and what factors make the process go faster or slower, to providing answers to common composting problems, this guide gives you the information you need to pick the right system and get started composting today.

By the end of the book, you will know the different types of composting and how they work, the benefits and drawbacks of each, the different types of composting systems and which of those systems is best for you. You will also know what you can and can't compost and how to diagnose the most common backyard composting issues.

When you're finished reading, you will have the tools you need to start turning your kitchen scraps and yard waste into black gold!

Happy Growing!

Gaia Rodale

Composting 101

It is safe to say that composting has been a part of human culture since the first person intentionally planted a seed in the hopes that they could grow something edible. It is a basic agricultural practice that many of us are as unfamiliar with as we are with other things everyone used to understand like animal husbandry or how to make bread from scratch.

However, as more and more people choose the path of organic gardening to grow some or all of their own produce, the ability to create high quality compost is a skill many are seeking to learn. Composting is a simple process that takes organic material from plants and transforms it into soil-amending material called humus or compost. The process behind this transformation is decomposition.

Nature is a composting machine, and you can see examples of it at work all around. The leaves from last year's trees fall to the ground where they mix with other dead plant material, which when exposed to microorganisms, bugs, earthworms, water, and sunshine, decomposes, providing nutrients the tree that produced the leaves needs to continue growing.

The goal of active composting is to speed up the natural process that turns organic matter into humus by creating ideal conditions for the decomposition to take place. To this end, the composting process requires four main ingredients: organic matter, moisture, oxygen, and bacteria. When the right bacteria and insects have access to adequate water and oxygen, the decomposition process can be accelerated.

Composting works because of microorganisms that are already present in an average backyard and on kitchen and yard waste. These bacteria do all the work of transforming those scraps into humus and creating conditions that are optimal for them to grow and thrive. The other key players are the larger insects, bugs, and earthworms that also help to break materials down into humus.

Important Factors for Successful Composting

As you can see in nature, all organic material will eventually decompose on its own, but that can take a long time. This is why organic gardeners often create their own composting program. Increasing the speed of decomposition means creating the best possible conditions for the bacteria and microorganisms that do all the work. Your success in creating those ideal conditions depends on several factors which are explained below.

Carbon to Nitrogen Ratio

Not all organic materials are created equally. Some, like dead leaves and manure are high in carbon. In composting, these materials are called browns. Other organic materials, like grass clippings and produce scraps from the kitchen, provide a source of nitrogen and are called greens. The microorganisms that make composting work need both carbon and nitrogen to thrive. In basic terms, the carbon acts as their food and the nitrogen makes it possible for them to digest it.

Successful composting requires the right ratio of browns to greens. The ideal ratio depends on what type of composting you are using.

Surface Area

In order to speed up decomposition, the material added to the compost pile or bin needs to have the maximum amount of surface area. More surface area means more microorganisms and better aeration. The best way to do this is to shred, chop, or otherwise break up the material into smaller pieces. For example, if you have an apple that has gone bad, it will decompose faster if you chop it up into pieces before adding it to the compost than it will if you leave it whole.

Aeration

Another important factor in speeding decomposition is aeration, which basically means making sure that the pile of materials has adequate access to oxygen. The microorganisms that you want working on your compost are the ones that need oxygen to live and thrive. If the pile is too compact, microbial life won't be able to take hold and decomposition will slow. Additionally, the process of decomposition uses up the available oxygen which means that maintaining adequate oxygen requires the oxygen to be replenished. The best way to accomplish both goals is to turn the compost on a regular basis.

Turning the compost pile, which effectively means mixing the old material in with the new using a pitchfork or an aerator, adds oxygen to the composting material. Turning also helps integrate new materials into the pile and exposes them to the microbial life in the pile so that decomposition can begin.

Aeration of the compost materials can also happen through more natural means. If the composting process is working optimally, the heat generated by the decomposition will help move air through the pile. The heated air and other gases will rise, and clean air will be drawn in to replace it.

Moisture

In order to do their job, the microorganisms in the compost pile need water, as they cannot make use of the molecules from the organic matter unless they are dissolved in water. In order to ensure there is adequate moisture to speed decomposition, the composting material should be 40-60% water. If the moisture level drops below that, the process of decomposition will slow down as the microbial activity slows or goes dormant.

Lack of moisture in the compost material also affects the oxygen level of the pile, which in turn increases the chances for anaerobic decomposition. This is the type of decomp that causes the nasty smells we associate with garbage. If the compost pile is emitting a bad smell, it probably needs more water.

One way to determine if the material in your compost has enough water is called the squeeze test. A handful of compost material should have the same moisture content as a sponge that is wet but that has been wrung out. In other words, it shouldn't be dripping wet, but moisture should be readily present.

However, there is such a thing as too much moisture as well. If you find that your compost pile's water content is too high, add more dry materials to get back to the right level.

What Can You Compost

Nitrogens

- Algae, seaweed, and lake moss are full of nitrogen and are a good source of nutrients and minerals.
- Banana peels are a good source of nitrogen. Shred or chop them to break them down faster.
- Clover can provide extra nitrogen.
- Coffee grounds and filters are a great source of nitrogen and will attract lots of earthworms.
- Fresh flowers can be added as a nitrogen.
- Fruit peels and rinds (except limes) can be added as a source of nitrogen. Make sure you chop them up well before adding them.
- Green grass clippings are a good source of nitrogen.
- Hair can be added and provides a good source of nitrogen
- Hay provides nitrogen. It's best when it is dry and already starting to decompose.
- Manure from herbivores like cows, chickens, horses, pigs, and sheep can provide a good source of nitrogen.
- Vegetable pieces and peels can be added as a source of nitrogen.

Carbons

- Cardboard can be added as a carbon if you shred it up, but don't add too much, recycle it instead.
- Cornstalks and corn cobs provide carbon, but try to break them down by shredding or chopping to hasten decomp.

- Dryer lint can be used as a carbon. Just moisten it before adding it to the pile.
- Dried flowers can be added as a carbon.
- Dried or brown grass clippings can be added but need to be counted as a carbon.
- Clippings from hedges are a good carbon source, but break them down into small pieces before adding.
- Kelp provides carbon and is a good source of potassium. Use it sparingly, however.
- Leaves are a carbon source. Shred or chop them before adding.
- Newspaper can be added as a carbon source. Shred this before adding too.
- Nut shells can be added as a source of carbon. Chop them up to help break them down more quickly.
- Sawdust can be added and provides a good carbon source, but avoid using sawdust from kiln-dried wood.
- Shredded paper can be added as a carbon source.
- Pinecones and pine needles will both provide carbon. Chop or break them up to aid in decomp.
- Tea leaves are a source of carbon.

Neutrals

- Egg shells are a neutral material that can benefit the pile, just crush them before adding them because they break down very slowly.
- Wood ashes are neutral and can be added to the pile sparingly to aid with pest management.

Things that Should Not Go in the Compost

- Anything that is not biodegradable

- Ashes from coal or charcoal fires
- Cat droppings or litter containing cat waste
- Colored paper
- Dairy products
- Lime (the mineral not the fruit)
- Meat, fat, grease, oils, bones

Why Organic Gardeners Compost

When organic gardeners turn some of their kitchen scraps
and yard waste into compost, everyone wins. Composting is
the best way to naturally amend soil and to ensure it is packed
with the nutrients needed to grow a healthy organic garden.
In addition to creating healthier soil, it is also a form of
recycling, as all the waste that goes in the compost doesn't
end up in a landfill. The real question should be why would
an organic gardener not compost, when there are so many
benefits to doing something that is fairly easy to do.

Why Compost is Important in Organic Gardening

Compost is made up of organic matter that serves several
purposes in an organic garden. Even though it only accounts
for about 10% of the soil in the garden, it is essential to a
successful garden. Let's explore some of the reasons it is so
important.

Amending and Improving the Soil

One of the most important things the organic matter in
compost does is amend and improve the soil. Most people
think that means it is used instead of fertilizer. This is partly
true, but the soil amendment benefit goes beyond what
simply adding fertilizer would accomplish.
The organic matter in compost helps bind the particles in the
soil together is such a way that water and air can better move
within the soil. This helps ensure plants growing in that soil
have access to the air and water they need to thrive.
Additionally, when soil has a higher concentration of organic
matter it can better retain water, which means plants have
access to water longer regardless of external conditions.

Compost can transform problem soils like those that are
primarily clay or very sandy. Compost added to soil with a
high clay content makes the clay become lighter and better
aerated. Compost added to sandy soil significantly improves
water retention. It can also help achieve and maintain a
proper pH in the soil and can help cut back on soil erosion.

Replacing and Replenishing Nutrients

There is a reason many organic gardeners call compost black
gold. In addition to helping improve the structure of the soil,
it also adds nutrients and helps the soil hold more nutrients,
good news for plants. Another way that compost adds
nutrients to the soil is by providing a food source for
earthworms and other soil creatures. These critters eat the
organic matter in the compost and leave behind nutrient-rich
excretions that provide food for the plants.

Aids in Natural Disease and Pest Control

One of the other benefits composting can provide for your
garden is natural protection from diseases and pests.
Research has shown that when added to garden beds,
compost helps prevent some soil-borne disease. Additionally,
when soil is amended with compost, it produces healthier,
heartier plants, and when plants are healthy and strong, they
are more able to resist disease and pests and recover from any
damage caused.

Better for the Environment

Composting is just another form of recycling; it is just one
that you do yourself. The impact of backyard composting is
likely greater than you think. In most households, the
percentage of waste that goes in a landfill that could go in
compost is about 30%. This means that without making any
other changes, simply composting your kitchen scraps and

yard waste can cut back your contribution to the problem of waste management by 30%. Another study indicated that simply starting a backyard composting program would eliminate at least 700 pounds of material each year from landfills and incinerators.

When these wastes go into a landfill rather than a backyard compost pile, they break down more slowly than they would if they were composted. The entire process takes longer, and because decomposition is occurring in less than ideal conditions, it produces methane gas and other harmful byproducts. These same materials, composted in the backyard, create a healthy way to feed the soil in the garden or the yard.

Types of Composting

If you make a pile of compost material in your backyard and never look at it again, it will eventually decompose and be transformed into dirt. This is called passive composting and is one way of transforming those broccoli stems and egg shells into compost. However, most organic gardeners need their compost to change organic matter into humus much more quickly in order to meet the needs of their hungry garden. For this reason, most of what we call composting is actually "active composting." Essentially, we are taking action to help the compost transform more quickly.

There are a couple different types of active composting that can easily be accomplished in a backyard. The three most common are hot composting, cold composting, and vermicomposting which is composting with worms. There are benefits and drawbacks to each type. The one that is best for you may vary depending on your location, time, and needs.

Hot Composting

If you are looking for the fastest composting option, hot is the way to go. By taking this approach, you can have high-quality, ready-to-use compost in about 6-8 weeks. However, hot composting definitely takes more active time, energy, and attention.

To create a hot compost pile, compost material is collected until there is at least 27 cubic feet of material – a pile that is 3 feet by 3 feet by 3 feet or 5 feet at the base and 3 feet at the top. This is considered critical mass for a hot compost.

Once you have enough material, the pile is formed by mixing 1 part greens and 2 parts browns and piling it all together. If you have vegetable or fruit scraps, put them in the middle to keep animals from scavenging in your pile.

Next, make sure the pile has the right amount of moisture by
the squeeze test explained earlier in this guide. Having
ght amount of moisture is critical to creating the
vironment needed to produce the internal heat that gives
this type of composting its name. If the moisture level is off,
add more moisture or more dry material until it is right.
The microorganisms will get to work as soon as the
conditions are right. As they work to decompose the
materials in the pile, their bodies will produce heat, which
then heats the pile. The composition of the pile acts as an
insulator, keeping the heat in and helping keep the conditions
for decomposition ideal. Hot compost piles should have an
interior temperature of 120 degrees F to 150 degrees F.
In order to let the pile build up the internal temperature, hot
piles shouldn't be turned for the first two weeks. Once the
microorganisms have gotten to work, the pile should be
turned once a week, and the moisture level in the pile should
be checked regularly. The hot phase will last for about a
month. After that, the pile will cool to 80-110°F. The
compost is ready once the pile stops producing heat, and the
organic matter is no longer recognizable.
The primary benefits of hot composting are the speed with
which the compost is broken down and the ability of the heat
to kill any weed seeds and plant pathogens contained in the
base material. The main drawback of using hot composting
is that it takes more active time and attention from the
gardener to monitor the different factors in order to maintain
optimal conditions.

Cold Composting

Compost can also be created without the heat produced by
the decomposition process seen in hot composting.
Sometimes, even while attempting hot composting, the pile
simply won't produce the heat needed to achieve a hot pile.

This is often the case in small backyard compost piles, especially when people first begin to compost. The important thing to remember is that cold composting will result in the same high-quality compost as the hot method, it will just take longer. Some studies even indicate that the nutrient content of compost created with the cold method is actually higher than that found in hot compost.

Creating a cold compost pile is much easier than creating a hot one. Make a pile of the same materials you would use to build your hot pile. The right ratio for a cold pile is about 1 brown to 1 green. Turn the pile once every month or two. Add new materials to the top of the pile and add water as needed. After six months, the material at the bottom of the pile may be finished. However, it can take as long as two years for compost to be ready using this method.

The primary benefit of the cold compost method is that it is easy to start and doesn't require a lot of effort to maintain. The main drawbacks are that it can take up to two years for compost to be ready, and without the heat, weed seeds and plant pathogens are more likely to survive the composting process.

Worms

If you don't have room for a big pile of compost on your property or you are an urban dweller without access to a compost-appropriate location, you can still compost much of your kitchen waste through vermicomposting, which uses an indoor bin containing worms. A vermicomposting bin is small and easy to fit into a closet, pantry, garage, or even on a balcony. This type of composting makes the process available no matter how little outdoor space you have. Composting with worms has the same benefits of the other two types of composting, including finished compost that can be used for indoor plants, herb gardens, vertical gardens, or any other gardening endeavor.

Vermicomposting uses a specific kind of warm called a red wiggler. These worms are a little different than regular earthworms that like to burrow into soil. Red wigglers live on or near the surface of the soil where they can do their job as nature's recycling crew. This is why they are perfect for indoor composting in a vermicomposting bin.

Each red wiggler will eat half its weight in food every day and then excrete nutrient-dense granules called castings. Castings generally contain a more diverse microbe base than traditional compost and are beneficial in boosting resistance to many fungal diseases. If you have a traditional compost pile but struggle with fungal disease, starting a small vermicomposting bin for use on those areas can help harden plants against fungal disease.

For a household of 2-4 people, a vermicomposting bin that holds 14 gallons of material should be enough to handle a normal amount of kitchen scraps. Vermicomposting bins can be purchased or easily made at home by using a plastic tub or by building a box.

To build your own bin from plastic or untreated wood, you need to drill 30 evenly spaced ½ inch holes in the bottom of the bin. Then do the same for the lid. Next, drill two rows of ventilation holes evenly spaced about 1.5 inches apart all the way around the bin. Start the first row three to four inches below the top edge of the bin. Place the second row about two inches below the first row.

In addition to your drilled bin, you will need a tray to go under the bin and a way to elevate the bin off the tray to allow for air flow. One easy way to do this is with small bricks. The purpose of the tray is to capture any liquid that drains from the bin, so it needs to be large enough to accomplish that goal.

You will want to locate your bin somewhere that it won't freeze but where it will stay under about 75° F. The bin should not be in direct sunlight.

In the bottom of the bin, create the first layer of bedding for the worms with strips of wet paper that have been wrung out and then "fluffed". This layer should take up about two thirds of the space in the bin. Add dry leaves and a cup of organic garden soil to the top. The bedding and leaves are similar to the red wigglers preferred habitat, and the soil helps them digest the kitchen scraps while also adding some helpful microbes to the mix.

Your bin is now ready for the red wigglers. You can find red wigglers at some home and garden shops or you can order them online. You will need a pound of worms to process about 3.5 pounds of scraps a week. The easiest way to determine how much waste you produce, and therefore how many worms you need, is to keep track of all the kitchen waste that would go in the worm bin for a week or two and use that as your gauge. You can always add more worms if you produce more waste than the worms can handle.

When you add your worms, spread them throughout the bin and then get started feeding them. The following can go in the bin, buried under the bedding:

- Fruit and veggie scraps (be cautious of adding too many citrus peels which can make the bin and bedding too acidic)
- Coffee grounds and filters
- Teabags
- Eggshells

Avoid anything that is cooked, oils, greases, meat, dairy products, and anything with spices.

A bin of this size can be turned into usable compost in about 12 weeks. Once the paper bedding has been broken down, simply move all the material in the bin to one half of the bin and build out new bedding in the other half. From this point forward, only add food to the side with new bedding. Over the next two to four weeks, the worms will migrate from the finished compost to the side with the new bedding. You can now remove the finished compost and build out new bedding on that side of the bin.

Creating Your Composting System

Although we have been talking about composting using "piles" so far, there are a few different types of composting systems that can be used for backyard composting. Most options can be built at home with simple materials or purchased from a store. The type of system that is best for you will depend on factors like what kind of space you have available and whether or not you are likely to experience problems with rodents or other wildlife. However, regardless of what kind of system you choose, the principles of each type of composting remain the same.

Piles

The most common composting system used by backyard gardeners is the compost pile. Used for both hot and cold composting, the pile is just that, a pile of material that is watered, turned, and eventually decomposes down into compost. For some gardeners, this pile is simply a pile somewhere in their yard or garden.

Others, especially those who practice cold composting, may use a fenced in or partially enclosed area that may be divided into two or more sections. The sections are used to separate partially decomposed material from full decomposed/curing material from new material that is being added to the pile. This method makes it possible to have a continuous input of new material while also producing finished compost on a regular basis.

Because the pile method means having a pile of kitchen and yard waste in the yard, it can attract rodents and other wild critters. If this is a problem, a more enclosed system is probably a better fit for you. You may also want to consider a combined system which is discussed later in this chapter.

Direct or Trench Composting

Another method favored by backyard composters and organic gardeners is called direct composting or trench composting. In this kind of system, kitchen scraps and compostable material isn't saved in a pile or added to a bin, it is buried in trenches or holes through the garden bed. Often done in the fall or early spring, the direct compost system gets the decomposing material directly into the soil as it breaks down.

Another way to do this with yard waste and straw or hay is to use these materials as the mulch for the paths throughout the garden. In the spring, they will have broken down and you will have a rich layer of compost to dig up and use throughout your garden beds.

Bins

In addition to using bins for worm composting as outlined in the previous chapter, bins can also be used for more traditional composting. Commercially available composting bins can make composting kitchen scraps easy and removes the need for a somewhat unsightly pile. This system is also beneficial for those who have problems with critters getting into their compost.

Composting bins are easy to make and can be made from almost anything. You can easily find instructions online for making your own bin from trash barrels, pallets, a plastic tub, or almost any other material. The key to remember in constructing your own bin is that the composting process requires moisture and air, so drainage and ventilation holes will be crucial to whatever design you choose.

One of the biggest challenge of using a compost bin is getting the composting material turned inside the bin often enough to provide adequate aeration for decomposition. Many purchased bins are too thin to make turning with a shovel or pitchfork practical, and many who use bins simply let the material decompose more slowly rather than trying to find a practical way of turning it inside the bin.

The other drawback of using a bin is that you will eventually end up with finished compost at the bottom and compost at various stages of decomposition piled on top of it. Most commercial bins provide a port or door at the bottom of the bin to extract the finished compost, but, as with turning, this often sounds much easier than it is in reality. Some organic gardeners simply dump the bin in their garden bed, separate the finished compost from the unfinished compost, replace the unfinished compost in the bin, and spread the finished compost where it is needed. This is a viable workaround that helps solve this problem, but it can be labor intensive and tedious.

If you are designing and building your own composting bin, make sure to take these two common problems into account as part of your design. Another way around these problems is to use a composting bin for kitchen scraps as part of a combination system which is covered later in this chapter.

Tumblers

For almost any organic gardener, a composting tumbler is the end-all, be-all composting system available. Unfortunately it is also the most expensive way to compost. These systems generally consist of a drum that is elevated off the ground using a stand that makes it possible to turn the drum. Turning the drum turns and aerates the compost inside.

Most drum tumblers have at least two compartments inside the drum. This makes it possible to be working on two batches of compost in differing stages of decomposition at the same time. This can help make up for the somewhat limited capacity of the tumblers which hold less than half the volume needed to make a hot pile work and somewhat less than most commercially available bins.

The frequent turning of the compost made possible by the elevated design of a tumbler composter paired with the insulated interior that helps keep the heat in makes it possible to complete a batch of compost in six to eight weeks. Despite the fact that it is more expensive to make or buy, a drum tumbler is well worth the cost. People who struggle with pests, like fire ants, or who are located in rural areas with lots of local wildlife may find an enclosed tumbler helps keep these unhelpful creatures away from their scraps and compost.

Combination Systems

For some organic gardeners, a system that utilizes only one type of composting isn't sufficient, so they create a system that utilizes more than one type of composting. The most common example of this is seen with gardeners who either can't put raw kitchen waste in a compost pile because of critters and rodents or who prefer not to because it is somewhat unsightly. These gardeners will often use a composting bin for kitchen waste in addition to a hot or cold pile.

In this kind of combination system, kitchen waste goes into the composting bin first. This may be located on a deck or in a garage, somewhere that is easily accessible from the kitchen all year round. The kitchen waste is left in the composting bin until it is partially broken down. Then it is added to the regular backyard pile where it can complete the decomposition process.

Organic gardeners may also use vermicomposting inside the house for some of their kitchen waste in addition to employing the other types of composting for other compostable materials. The bottom line is that you can use whichever composting types and methods you need to in order to create a system that works for you and your composting needs.

Implementing Your Composting System

Getting started with composting is easy, and as you learn what works and what doesn't, you will be able to refine your overall system in order to meet your composting goals. The most important thing to remember is that your ultimate goal is to speed up the natural process of decomposition. As long as you are focused on achieving that goal, everything will fall into line as you work the kinks out in your system.

Pick a Place to Start

The first step is to decide which kind of composting you want to start out with. If you have the room to do it, I recommend starting with a hot or cold pile because they are the easiest to manage. If you have the money, start with a tumbler because it makes the entire process easier. Just keep in mind that it may take a little time to get the hang of whichever type of composting you decide to start with. I will say that you are better off starting with one type of composting, even if you are planning to use a combination system, so that you can get used to the process before adding any complexity.

Get Your System Set Up

Once you know what you want to do, it's time to create a plan to build out your system and get some compost started. The first consideration is location. If you have opted for a pile, pick a spot that is close to your garden. Remember, every pound of compost you produce is going to end up in those garden beds so closer composting means less manual labor later on.

If you are using a bin or a tumbler, you are still better off locating it in or near the garden to make things easier. The only exceptions to this would be a vermicompost bin, which is likely to be located inside the house, and a kitchen-specific bin that is acting as an interim stop in your composting system. Both of these can be located closer to the kitchen for easier use.

Once you have your location, it is time to build out whatever system you have selected. You may be putting up a three section pile enclosure using cinder blocks or making your own composting bin. Whatever system you have selected, now is the time to get it built or bought and put it in.
In most areas, you shouldn't have to search too hard or purchase anything extra to make your composting endeavor successful. The obvious exception here is the purchase of red wigglers if you are vermicomposting. For the other types of systems, you should have enough dead leaves, coffee grounds, hedge clippings, and kitchen scraps to get your compost going without having to supplement with purchased materials. Just remember to keep the ratio between browns and greens right to get the best results.

Manage Your Microbials

Once your system is built out and the process has started, do your part to keep the microbial life, insects, fungi, and other decomposers working as hard as they can. Turning the pile is crucial to ensuring that the pile is aerated and the microorganisms have access to the oxygen they need to break down the material in the compost. Check the moisture level regularly to ensure that the pile is wet enough without becoming too wet for optimal decomposition. Keep the ratio of greens to browns right, and your system should be well on its way to producing high-quality compost in no time at all.

Another way to support the microorganisms and other life in your composting system is by providing them with a diverse food source. Each different type of material that you add to the composting process will bring with it new microbial life. This only makes the composting system stronger and more efficient. Try to choose from a range of materials in both the brown and green areas for the optimal results.

How Long Will it Take

The type of system you build will determine how long it will take to have finished compost that you can use. Using a well-seasoned tumbler can take as little as six weeks. Hot piles can take eight weeks. Bins and vermicomposting often take three to four months to produce finished compost, and cold composting can take anywhere from six months to two years.

If your pile seems to be taking longer than it should, you can try the following things to speed up the process:

- Add more green material, because too much brown will slow the process down.
- Make the pile bigger or smaller. This is especially true with hot piles which have an optimal size for a reason.
- Shred, chop, or otherwise break the material down more that is going into the pile or bin before adding it in order to increase the surface area.
- Turn the pile more often, since more aeration equals faster decomposition.
- Check the moisture level often. A pile or bin that is too wet or not wet enough will break down more slowly than a pile with adequate moisture.

Troubleshooting

Here are a couple of the most common problems organic gardeners encounter with their composting systems and the answers you need to solve them.

Problem #1: My composting pile is too wet, soggy, or seems to be slimy.

If you notice that your compost pile seems to be a cold, wet, soggy, or slimy mess, there is definitely something impeding the natural decomposition process. Since the goal of composting is to accelerate that process, start by checking the main requirements needed for composting to work.
First, make sure you are aerating the pile often enough to support the microorganisms that are doing all the work. Start turning the pile every one to two weeks, and see if that corrects the problem.

Second, it may be that there is simply too much moisture in the pile. If you have had a particularly rainy season, check the moisture level in the pile. Add more dry material if it seems too wet. You may have to check the moisture level more frequently if you are getting more rain than normal.

Third, your pile may not have enough nitrogen-rich materials to decompose as quickly as it should be. Try boosting the amount of greens that are going into the pile, and see if that corrects the problem.

One other thing to check would be the composition of the pile. If there is a layer of heavy or thick material that holds a lot of water on the top – like hay or leaves that haven't been shredded, that layer may be pressing down on the pile and preventing the center of the pile from getting enough oxygen for those microorganisms to do their work. Turn the pile and try to alleviate that heavy burden by breaking up some of that material.

Lastly, if your pile contains a lot of veggie scraps, which have a high water content, it can make your pile slimy. You need to balance out all those wet veggies with some bulkier, drier materials to help balance out the extra moisture.

Problem #2: My compost seems to always be dried out.

If you live in a location without much rainfall, you may find it challenging to keep your compost wet enough naturally to promote ideal decomposition conditions. If this is the case, you may need to start watering your compost the same way you water your garden.

Remember, your goal is to have the material in your pile or bin be about as wet as a sponge that has been wrung out. Start watering the compost, and then regularly check the moisture levels so that you can determine how much water needs to be added to the pile to maintain the right water level. If you have to water your pile to get the moisture level right, start by watering the top, then turning, then watering a little more, than turning it in order to ensure the entire pile is getting enough water. Once you get the pile wet enough and the microbial life starts working, make sure you don't let it dry out again.

Problem #3: I have bugs in my compost, is that bad?

There will almost always be bugs in your compost, unless it is in an enclosed tumbler, so just having bugs in the pile isn't necessarily a bad thing. Almost any bug you see in your compost is actually helping to break things down. However, certain bugs can indicate that your pile isn't working properly and some can become problematic if they are not removed from the finished compost before it is used in garden beds.

You are likely to find pill bugs, sow bugs, ants, and earwigs amongst the bug population of your compost pile. All of these bugs are attracted to decaying refuse and will infiltrate your pile if it isn't too hot for them. If you are using the cold composting method, these bugs are likely to be there lending a hand, and there isn't much you can do to get rid of them. If you are using the hot composting method, the presence of these bugs means your pile isn't hot enough. These bugs won't stick around if the pile gets up to 120°F.

The real problem with having these bugs in your compost is that if they are still there when you move the compost to the garden beds, they can do some pretty significant damage to the roots and leaves of your seedlings. If you have finished compost that still has these bugs in it, lay out a tarp or a piece of plastic somewhere in direct sunlight. Spread the compost in a thin layer over the tarp, and leave it for a couple hours. The bugs will abandon the compost to get out of the sunlight.

Problem #5: My compost pile smells like a landfill.

If your compost pile smells like something is rotting in it, this is a sure sign that there is not enough oxygen in the pile to support the kind of microorganisms you want. The smell means anaerobic decomposition is taking place. This is the kind of decomp that happens when there isn't enough oxygen. The material in the pile will eventually decompose and break down to humus, but it will go much more slowly, and you will have to deal with that smell.

To fix this problem, try turning the pile more often. If that doesn't help, you may need to rebuild the pile in order to create layers that allow adequate oxygen for the microbial life you want.

Conclusion

I hope you found this guide useful, and that it helped you decide which type of composting and what kind of composting system are right for your garden.

With the information provided here, you have the instructions you need to build your first composting system, optimize the decomposition process, and handle any common problems that occur.

By implementing your own composting system, you will be able to continuously build up the quality of your soil. After reading this guide, you now know:

- Why composting is important to organic gardeners
- The most important factors for successful composting
- What can be composted and what can't
- The difference between hot and cold composting
- What vermicomposting is and when it is beneficial
- The different types of composting systems
- How long it takes to create high quality compost
- How to solve some of the most common composting problems

This guide provided the information you need to pick the right composting system for your garden, build it out, and manage it to maximize the composting process. From outlining the different ways to compost to explaining how composting works, everything you need to turn kitchen scraps and yard waste into humus is on these pages.

Now that you are ready to start building your pile or filling your bin, it is time to get your hands in the dirt and make something happen.

Happy Growing!

Gaia Rodale

Check out some of Gaia's other books!!

http://www.amazon.com/dp/B00L1WBQW2

http://www.amazon.com/dp/B00KGLRRP4

http://www.amazon.com/dp/B00KNFAWKU

http://www.amazon.com/dp/B00L6EK8WY

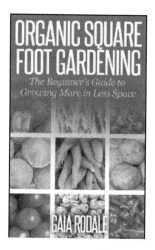

http://www.amazon.com/dp/B00JSA2JVG

http://www.amazon.com/dp/B00KE8QM28

http://www.amazon.com/dp/B00KFXB7ZY

http://www.amazon.com/dp/B00J7ZUZOA

Made in the USA
Columbia, SC
14 December 2017